One Land, Many Cultures

Maureen Picard Robins

rourkeeducationalmedia.com

Teacher Notes available at
rem4teachers.com

www.rourkeeducationalmedia.com

PHOTO CREDITS: Cover: © Diana Walters, © WendellandCarolyn; Title Page: © nicolesy, akkul; Page 3: © laflor; Page 4: © 3d_kot; Page 5: © JBryson; Page 6: © Carsten Reisinger; Page 7: Kevin Carden ©; Page 9: © Michael Flippo; Page 11: © ; Gary Hathaway; Page 13: © inhauscreative; Page 14: © LivingImages, Skypixel; Page 15: © selimaksan; Page 17: © plherrera; Page 18: © lisafx, YinYang; Page 19: © DougSchneiderPhoto, Jose Gil; Page 20: © asiseeit; Page 21: © JodiJacobson; Page 22: © GYI NSEA, WendellandCarolyn, Michael Flippo, Sven Klaschik; Page 23: © KentWeakley, Gary Hathaway, YinYang

Edited by: Precious McKenzie
Cover design by: Tara Raymo
Interior design by: Renee Brady

Library of Congress PCN Data

One Land, Many Cultures / Maureen Picard Robins
(Little World Social Studies)
ISBN 978-1-61810-143-3 (hard cover)(alk. paper)
ISBN 978-1-61810-276-8 (soft cover)
Library of Congress Control Number: 2011945870

Rourke Educational Media
Printed in the United States of America,
North Mankato, Minnesota

rourkeeducationalmedia.com

customerservice@rourkeeducationalmedia.com • PO Box 643328 Vero Beach, Florida 32964

The United States is one land but we have many **cultures**.

In my **neighborhood**, in New York City, I have friends from many different places. My friends come from China, Morocco, Colombia, Mexico, Jamaica, Egypt, and Poland.

Let's find where my friends came from on a map. Do you have friends who came from different parts of the world?

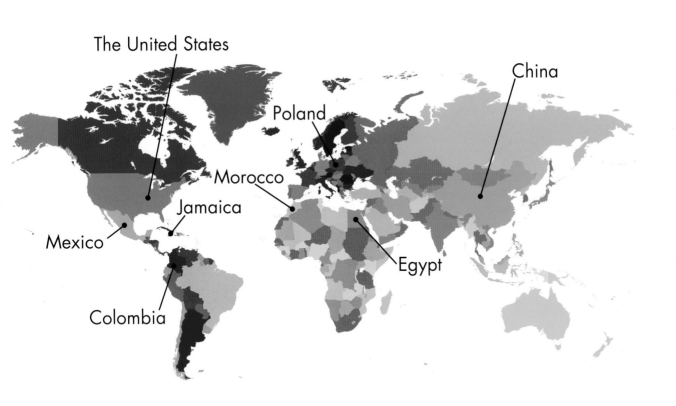

A new boy came to my class from Colombia, South America. He speaks Spanish. When we worked on the math problem of the week, we tried to help him with his English.

Can you see how far he **traveled** to get here? Let's look at the map.

The United States

Colombia

Sometimes my friend from China shares his vegetable rolls and wontons with me at lunch.

vegetable rolls

wontons

A wonton is a Chinese **dumpling**. A dough wrapping is stuffed with pork. It is often served in soup. The name wonton means swallowing a cloud.

One day another friend brought hummus and flatbread that his grandmother made. His family is from Egypt.

hummus

flatbread

The United States

Egypt

My teacher found out that we shared our lunches. That gave him an idea. He decided to give us a new math problem of the week.

Math Problem of the Week

How many different types of food would our class have if we celebrated with one dish from each of the cultures in our classroom?

Almost all of my friends have parents or grandparents who came from other countries. My friend, Nevaeh, came from Jamaica. Her family loves to make meat patties and codfish fritters.

meat patty   **codfish fritters**

My friend, Philip, told me his grandparents live in Chicago. Originally, they came from Poland.

Fun Fact

Pierogis are Polish-style dumplings. A dough pocket is stuffed with sauerkraut or potatoes and then fried.

My classmate, Juan, piped up and said his family came to the United States from Mexico. He loves to eat tamales, empanadas, and rice and beans.

Fun Fact

A tamale is a corn-based dough stuffed with meats or cheese and spices and then wrapped in a corn husk.

My friend, Fatima, is from Morocco.
She makes homemade peanut soup
with her family.

When we brought our different foods to school, twenty-five dishes overloaded the table! We had wontons, pierogis, empanadas, hummus, and so much more! Then we were able to solve our math problem of the week.

25 kids =

25 different types
of food

After trying lots of new foods, we learned the United States was made great by **immigrants**. Over the **history** of our country, people from many nations came to America for a better life and helped build this country.

Thanks to the many immigrants, past and present, we live in a land with many cultures.

Thanks!

Picture Glossary

 **cultures** (kuhl-churz): The word to describe a way of life, ideas, customs, and traditions of a group of people.

 **dumpling** (duhmp-ling): Cooks mix flour and water to form a dough which is cut and used to wrap meat, potato, or cheese. It is often served in soup.

 **history** (HISS-tuh-ree): When you study or learn about past events.

immigrants (im-uh-gruhntz): People who travel from one country to live permanently in another.

neighborhood (nay-bur-hud): The local area around your house or a small section of the city or town where you live.

traveled (TRAV-uld): When people have gone from one place to another.

Index

Websites

www.nytimes.com/interactive/2009/03/10/us/
   20090310-immigration-explorer.html

www.kids-cooking-activities.com/international-gourmet-recipes.html

ngm.nationalgeographic.com/map/atlas

About the Author

Maureen Picard Robins writes poetry and books for kids and adults. She is an assistant principal at a New York City middle school. She lives in one of the five boroughs of New York City with her husband and daughters.

Ask The Author!
www.rem4students.com